Beauty is not caused. It is.

Emily Dickinson

Blue Mountain Arts®

Bestselling Titles

By Susan Polis Schutz:
To My Daughter, with Love, on the Important Things in Life
To My Son with Love

By Douglas Pagels:
30 Beautiful Things That Are True About You
42 Gifts I'd Like to Give to You
100 Things to Always Remember... and One Thing to Never Forget
May You Always Have an Angel by Your Side
To the One Person I Consider to Be My Soul Mate

Is It Time to Make a Change?
by Deanna Beisser

I Prayed for You Today
To the Love of My Life
by Donna Fargo

Anthologies:
Always Believe in Yourself and Your Dreams
For You, My Daughter
Friends for Life
Hang In There
I Love You, Mom
I'm Glad You Are My Sister
The Joys and Challenges of Motherhood
The Language of Recovery
Marriage Is a Promise of Love
Teaching and Learning Are Lifelong Journeys
There Is Greatness Within You, My Son
Think Positive Thoughts Every Day
Thoughts to Share with a Wonderful Teenager
True Wealth
With God by Your Side ...You Never Have to Be Alone
You're Just like A Sister to Me

I Am Beautiful

Affirmations for Women

Diane Mastromarino

Blue Mountain Press™
Boulder, Colorado

We wish to thank Susan Polis Schutz for permission to reprint the following poem that appears in this publication: "Give yourself the freedom to try out…." Copyright © 1989 by Stephen Schutz and Susan Polis Schutz. All rights reserved.

Library of Congress Control Number: 2005019941
ISBN: 0-88396-931-9

Certain trademarks are used under license.
BLUE MOUNTAIN PRESS is registered in U.S. Patent and Trademark Office.

Printed in the United States of America.
First Printing: 2005

 This book is printed on recycled paper.

This book is printed on fine quality, laid embossed, 80 lb. paper. This paper has been specially produced to be acid free (neutral pH) and contains no groundwood or unbleached pulp. It conforms with the requirements of the American National Standards Institute, Inc., so as to ensure that this book will last and be enjoyed by future generations.

Library of Congress Cataloging-in-Publication Data

I am beautiful : affirmations for women / [compiled by] Diane Mastromarino.
   p. cm.
  ISBN 0-88396-931-9 (trade pbk. : alk. paper) 1. Women—Psychology—Miscellanea. 2. Affirmations. I. Mastromarino, Diane, 1978- IV. Title.
HQ1206.I36 2005
158.1'28'082—dc22

                                  2005019941

Blue Mountain Arts, Inc.

P.O. Box 4549, Boulder, Colorado 80306

Introduction

We are strong, confident, and incredible. We are caring, nurturing, and kind. We are brave and brilliant and unbelievably beautiful. The problem is many times we lose sight of all these things and need to be reminded.

This book is for *those* times. Those moments when we lose ourselves trying to keep up with the world. Those days when we feel we can't do anything right. Those mornings when our pants are a little too snug around the waist and those nights when there's just not enough time to get everything done. Those few seconds when we catch our tired reflection in the mirror and aren't sure exactly who's staring back. This book is for all those times when we just don't feel our very best.

A collection of affirmations is very different from other books. It doesn't have to be read from beginning to end to grasp the concept or gain a new understanding. *I Am Beautiful* can be picked up at any time and opened to any page. Below the affirmations are a few ways for you to discover in your own life your own beautiful self. Try them out or create your own. Enjoy… and remember, you are beautiful!

I... do not know anyone who is able to love herself who does not grow beautiful.

Kaylan Pickford

I am beautiful.

Part of being beautiful is the knowledge that I am not just saying those words, but truly believing them. I must look at myself through tender eyes and allow myself to feel loved. I must be less critical and more compassionate. No matter how I am feeling or how bad my day is going, I must always remember that I deserve to be loved.

Each morning I will smile at the woman in the mirror instead of scowling. I will be sensitive to her needs and treat her with kindness. I will be proud of her accomplishments and accepting of her faults. I will allow her to be herself. She is me and I am beautiful.

Today I will pay myself a compliment...
and believe it!

Today I will give myself a big hug.

Today I will only use positive words
to describe myself and my life.

A beautiful thing is never perfect.

Egyptian Proverb

I am beautiful.

I know that I am not perfect. I acknowledge this with an open mind and an open heart. There may be parts of me that I would change if I could, but I accept that some things in life cannot be changed. This acceptance isn't easy, but it makes me a stronger person. I will try my best not to dwell on my imperfections in resentment or frustration. Instead I will see them as just one part of a beautiful whole.

Perfection is overrated. If everyone in this world were perfect, we would all be exactly the same. It is the very things that make me different that make me beautiful. I am unique in my appearance, in my wisdom, and in my emotions. I create my own style, my own rhythm, and my own way of being. These are the things that set me apart, the things that make me irreplaceable. These are the things that make me beautiful.

Today I will write down three things I like about myself.

Today I will frame a picture of myself to put in my bedroom.

Today I will start a gratitude journal.

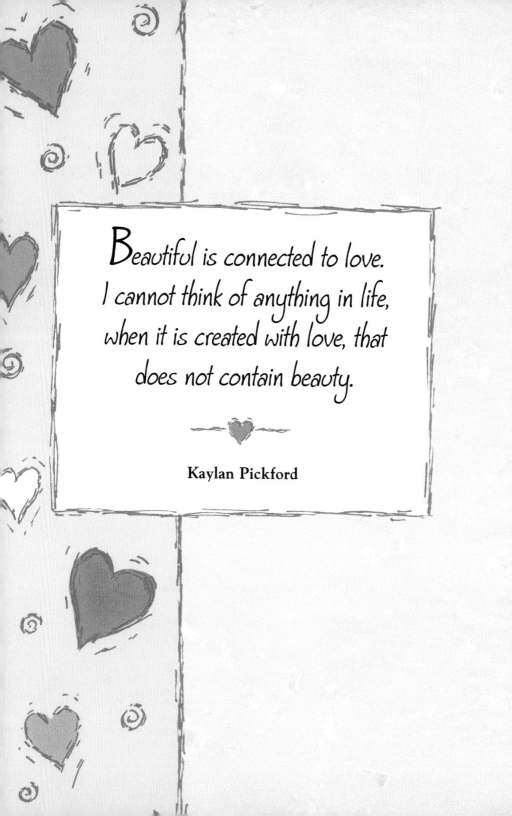

Beautiful is connected to love. I cannot think of anything in life, when it is created with love, that does not contain beauty.

Kaylan Pickford

I am beautiful.

I am capable of loving and of being loved. I deserve nothing less. I will open myself up to the giving and receiving of love and to all the possibilities offered to me. It is only then that love can enter into my life. A loving heart seeks another loving heart. A welcoming smile seeks a kindred soul. I embrace love with an open mind and an open heart.

Love is created through friendship, trust, and loyalty. It is a gift that should be appreciated and treated kindly. My heart is delicate and those whom I share it with must respect it as I do. Love cannot be forced or tied down. Like air, it must be able to flow freely both into and out of my life.

Love is the incredible experience of getting to know someone, letting that person know me, and making a connection that will affect both our lives. Love is a beautiful gift.

Today I will join a community group
to help me meet new people.

Today I will tell someone that I love them.

Today I will call someone I think about often.

There Is So Much Beauty

There is beauty
in so many unrecognized places.
It's a different beauty than
what you find in magazines,
where the faces all become
the same page after page.
Neither is it about shapes or fabrics
or cut and color.

Beauty is how you invite people
into your life and your heart no matter what;
when you laugh or cry with your whole self,
just because that's how you feel.

Beauty is the way you move
when you think no one is watching
and you forget the shadows
of "should" and "supposed to."

Beauty is courage, energy,
    hope, and grace.

Beauty is you —
    just the <u>way</u> you are.

Sue Gillies-Bradley

When a woman conceives
her true self, a miracle occurs
and life around her begins.

Marianne Williamson

I Am Beautiful

I am beautiful.

Sometimes I lose myself in what the world expects of me. There is so much pressure to be and act a certain way, to adhere to the standards others create. I will try not to conform to what I "should be" according to magazine articles and television shows. I will ask myself, "What is my motivation?" "Who am I doing this for?"

I will not walk through my days in black and white; I will leap through life in brilliant color: red and yellow and turquoise and green. I will create my own box and step outside it as I wish. I will wear what I want to wear and dance how I want to dance. I will shout from the rooftops, "World, here I am!" I will let everyone know my presence is worth noticing.

*Today I will wear the brightest colored article
of clothing in my closet.*

*Today I will steer clear of magazines that tell me
how I should be.*

Today I will be happy with myself just the way I am.

I Am Beautiful When...

I am beautiful when I step out of my comfort zone and explore new horizons.

I am beautiful when I allow myself to be challenged... when I embrace new experiences with open arms.

I am beautiful when I learn something new.

I am beautiful when I wear blue jeans
and an oversized T-shirt.

I am beautiful when my hair's a mess
and I haven't put my makeup on yet.

I am beautiful when I'm authentic…
when my mind and body are at ease
and I am completely myself.

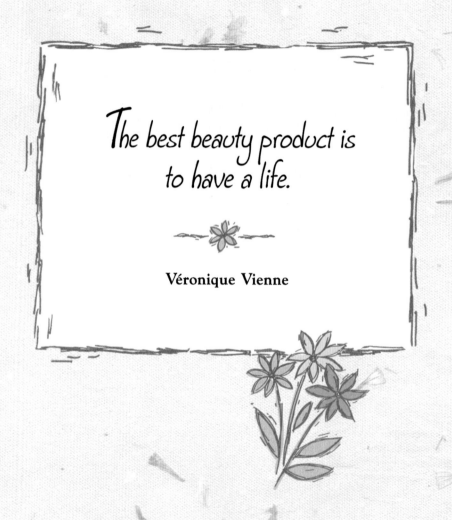

The best beauty product is
to have a life.

Véronique Vienne

I am beautiful.

I am a woman on the go. I have a cause. I am here for a reason. The world needs me and I need the world. I wasn't born just to take up space; I was born to make a difference.

When I die I want to be remembered as a woman who led a meaningful life — a woman who took risks, a woman who made statements. I make every day count, even if it's just in one tiny way. Whether it's finishing a book or saving the world, there is always a goal ahead of me. I don't jump on bandwagons or follow the crowd. I have great opinions and even greater dreams. Every morning I wake up, I have the choice of what is to come. I choose to be beautiful by leading a beautiful life.

Today I will start a project I've been putting off.

Today I will do something unexpected.

*Today I will make a list of all the things
I want to accomplish in the next ten years.*

Know your voice is your essential,
number-one treasure. Let it out.
A voice hates being boxed up.
It shrinks if you box it up.

❀

Naomi Shihab Nye

I am beautiful.

My opinions and feelings matter. My questions deserve to be answered. By speaking up and being present, I am making a contribution to the world, and that is a remarkable gift that only I can give. My voice can make a big difference in my life and in the lives of others.

There will be times when speaking up is hard to do, but these are the times when my voice matters the most. Others may criticize me or question what I am saying, but it doesn't matter as long as my words come from my heart. My voice is powerful and significant and beautiful. My voice deserves to be heard.

*Today I will write a letter to the editor
about something I believe in.*

Today I will ask a question to learn something new.

Today I will look someone in the eye and voice my opinion.

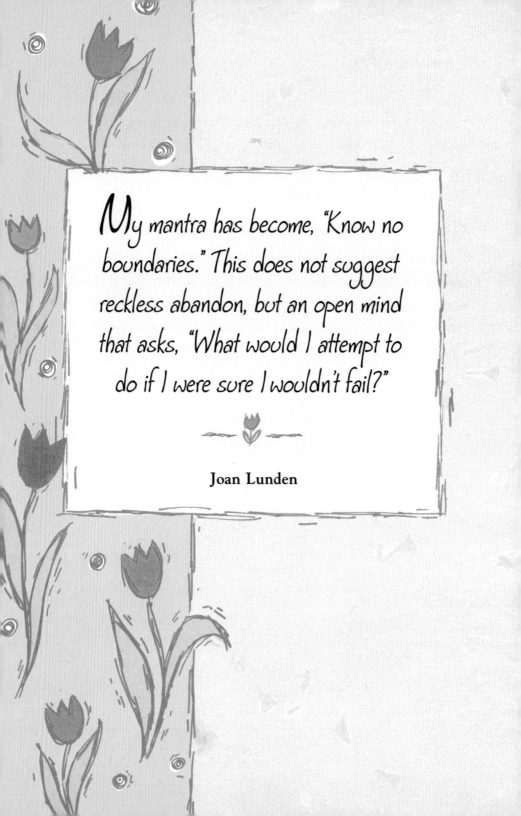

My mantra has become, "Know no boundaries." This does not suggest reckless abandon, but an open mind that asks, "What would I attempt to do if I were sure I wouldn't fail?"

Joan Lunden

I am beautiful.

The sky is my limit. I will reach up to it with my arms wide open and all the courage my heart can muster. I will be fearless because fear is nothing but an obstacle begging to be conquered. What is the worst that can happen? I may fail or falter, but not without learning something new... not without gaining greater insight into the world in which I live.

I know there will be times when doubt creeps into my view. There will be small voices that sometimes say, "No, you can't," but I will rise above them. I will ask myself, "What is it that holds me back?" I will remind myself that I am capable and able. I am courageous, I am beautiful, and there's no limit to what I can do.

Today I will attempt something I failed at in the past.

Today I will book a trip to a place I've always wanted to go.

Today I will do something I'm afraid to do.

It Has to Do...

It has to do with knowing the person you've been, the person you are, the person you want to become. It has to do with keeping yourself in perspective.

It has to do with recognizing what you want and knowing how to get it.

It has to do with believing in yourself.

It has to do with faith and trust — faith in something or someone bigger than you are; trust in the belief that anything is possible.

It has to do with love....

It has to do with finding positive impressions on which to build....

It has to do with tolerance. See yourself as you wish to be seen; see others as they wish to be seen; help the rest of us to see the difference.

It has to do with kindness. Be aggressively kind and it will find you on the rebound.

It has to do with folly. Don't be afraid to cut loose, have fun, defy convention....

It has to do with overcoming your past, anticipating your future, and sidestepping the obstacles in between....

It has to do with rejecting some of our more commonly held notions of beauty in favor of the ones that make sense....

It has to do with living at the edges of opportunity, and knowing when to look over the side.

It has to do with resisting the impulse to fit the mold....

It has to do with keeping one foot in reality and the other in fantasy.

It has to do with accepting change.

It has to do with understanding what works, and what doesn't. Shadow your flaws, showcase your gifts, and give it your best shot.

It has to do with reason. Think it through.

It has to do with balance. Adjust your levels of work and play; diet and exercise; rest and motion....

It has to do with forgiveness....

It has to do with respect. For yourself. For others. For new ideas....

It has to do with living. It's not enough to go through the motions. Give yourself over to life and see what happens.

It has to do. Period.

Emme

The ones who survive in life do it by hammering at it one day at a time. You do what you have to do to get through today, and that puts you in the best place tomorrow.

Oprah Winfrey

I am beautiful.

I am strong. I am wise. I am brave. I accept that some days will be harder than others. There will be days filled with tummy aches and heartaches and headaches. There will be days when things don't go as planned. I will get through these days the best that I can. I will keep my chin up and my eyes focused on where I am going. I will believe in myself, and I will not let other people bring me down.

The rainy days teach me to appreciate the sunshine. I need them to grow stronger and wiser and braver. I need them to become more and more beautiful. With one deep breath at a time, I will move through today into tomorrow… and every tomorrow will be the best day yet.

Today I will have a good cry.

Today I will treat myself to something special.

Today I will breathe deeply and let the negative energy flow out of me.

I Am Beautiful When...

I am beautiful when I make wishes on falling stars and truly believe they can come true.

I am beautiful when I am hopeful about what is to come... when I embrace the future with open arms, and welcome what it has to offer me.

I am beautiful when I close my eyes, curl into bed, and leave my day behind me.

I am beautiful when I am honest with myself and others.

I am beautiful when I speak the words that are in my heart... when I stand up for what I believe in.

I am beautiful when I am confident.

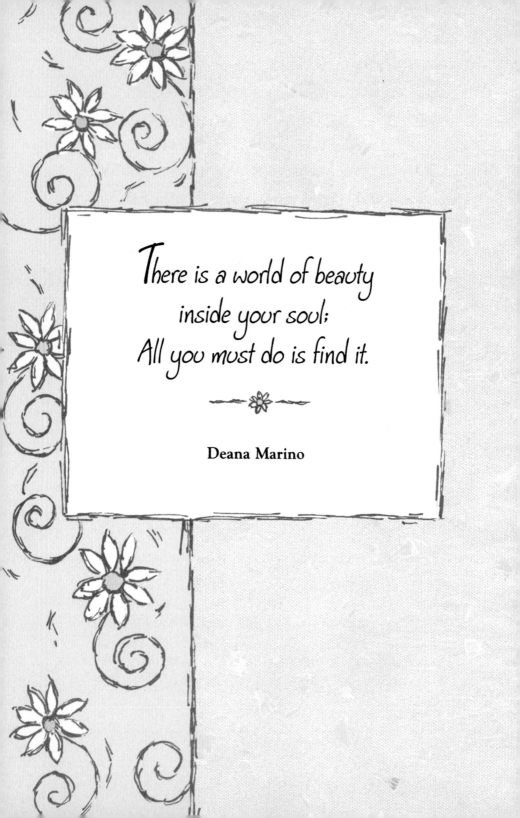

There is a world of beauty
inside your soul;
All you must do is find it.

Deana Marino

I am beautiful.

I embrace solitude and accept the comfort of being alone. I know the importance of rediscovering myself — analyzing my needs, decisions, and choices. Am I staying true to myself? Am I following the career path that is fulfilling to me? Is the lifestyle I have chosen really mine? These are questions only I can answer when I am completely alone with myself.

I will take time to get to know myself better — to experience my emotions, appreciate my body, and reconnect with my spirit. With just myself present, I will let everything flow freely — my voice, my emotions, my entire being. I will cry if I need to or laugh out loud. I will find a relaxing place to be one with my thoughts. This is my time to acknowledge my hopes, dreams, and desires and bring them to the surface. This is my time to discover all the beauty I hold within me.

Today I will discover myself through meditation.

Today I will plan a weekend retreat.

Today I will have a conversation with myself that begins with, "If I could live my life over again, I would..."

31

Beautiful Women

Beautiful women are those who know the road ahead will be strewn with obstacles, but they still choose to walk it because it's the right one for them.

Beautiful women are those who make mistakes, who admit to them, learn from that failure, and then use that knowledge.

Beautiful women are easily hurt, but they still extend their hearts and hands, knowing the risk and accepting the pain when it comes.

Beautiful women are sometimes beat down by life, but they still stand back up and step forward again.

Beautiful women are afraid. They face the fear and move ahead to the future, as uncertain as it can be.

Beautiful women are not those who succeed the first time. They're the ones who fail time and again, but still keep trying until they succeed.

Beautiful women face the daily trials of life, sometimes with a tear, but always with their heads high as the new day dawns.

Brenda Hager

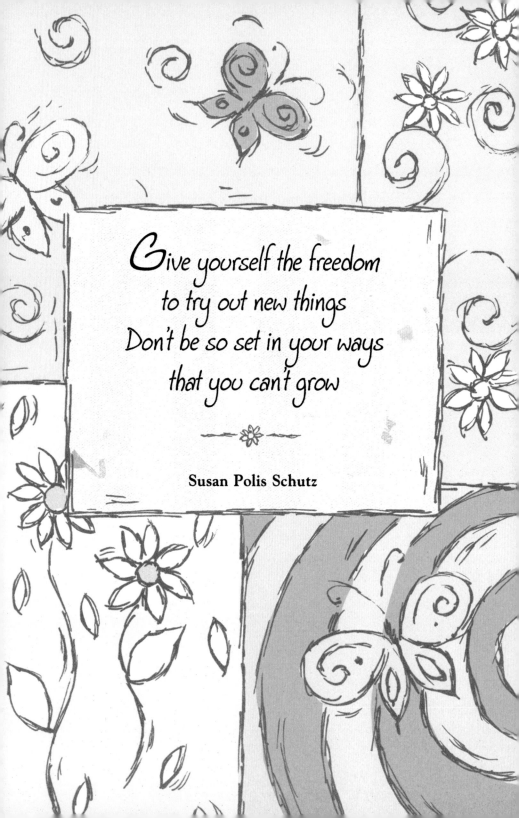

Give yourself the freedom
to try out new things
Don't be so set in your ways
that you can't grow

❀

Susan Polis Schutz

I am beautiful.

Life is constantly changing in small and great ways. People come and go, and sudden circumstances unfurl. I can choose to be stagnant, or I can ride life like the wind. I choose to embrace my world with open arms, to stretch myself beyond my limits, and find goodness in transformation.

I will not dwell on past circumstances. I will keep focused on today and be fully present in the moment. I will look for wonder in unexpected places. Every day is a chance to grow and a chance to rediscover myself and others. I will ask the questions: What does the world have to offer me? What will I do with what is set before me? And my answer will be: Great, marvelous, fabulous things that only I am capable of doing.

Today I will get a dramatic haircut.

Today I will rearrange my furniture.

Today I will begin to live a healthier lifestyle.

When my body is strong,
I also feel powerful
in other areas of my life.

☆

Serena Williams

I am beautiful.

My body is my responsibility, and it is up to me to treat it with care. I will try my best to eat healthy foods, exercise regularly, and laugh often. I will surround myself with good people, good thoughts, and great energy.

My health is a top priority. I will be aware of what I put into my body and how it affects me. I will use sunscreen on hot days and button my coat in the winter. I will listen to my body and respect its wishes. I am my body, and my body is beautiful.

Today I will go on a long walk and stop to smell the flowers.

Today I will eat a healthy snack.

Today I will quit a habit that is detrimental to me.

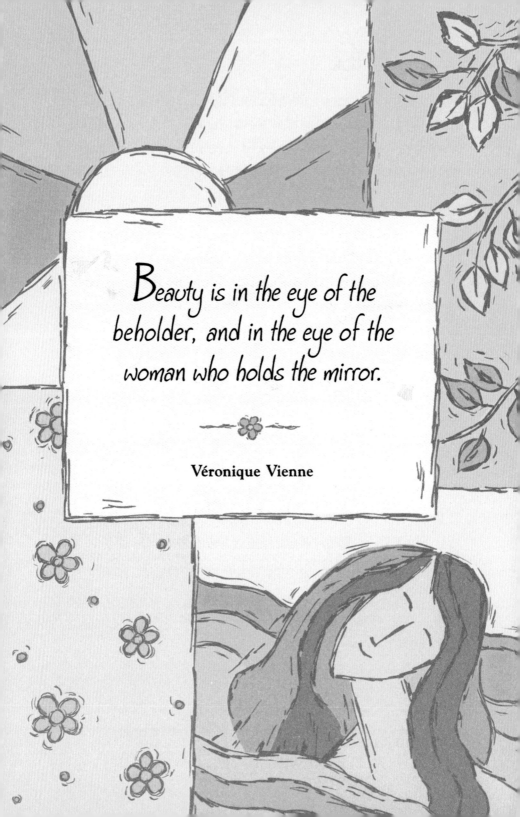

Beauty is in the eye of the beholder, and in the eye of the woman who holds the mirror.

Véronique Vienne

I am beautiful.

Some people will agree, and some may not. But all that matters is that I can say quietly to myself — and on better days, scream out loud — I am beautiful. I do not live by others' approval. I do not find the need to follow others' standards because I construct my own. I follow my heart where it leads me. I create my own destiny as well as the path that takes me to it.

I know that in the eye of each beholder, the opinion of beauty wavers. I will try my best to remember this always, and not lose myself in a quest to satisfy someone else's definition of beauty. I am better than that. I appreciate me for me, and in my life that is all that really matters.

Today I will choose what I wear
without contemplating what anyone else will think.

Today I will walk down the street with pride.

Today I will write myself a love poem.

Decide That You're Beautiful

🌀 *Decide that you're beautiful.* Let your quirks and imperfections be part of your beauty, like the models who turn a mole or a gap between their front teeth into a trademark. Keep reminding yourself that you're beautiful until you believe it. Once you do, other people will believe it too. When you get a compliment, accept it.

🌀 *Get healthy.* "Health and beauty," wrote Emerson, "are nature's gifts for living within her laws." Exercise, rest, and nutritious food are the raw materials for clear skin, sparkling eyes, shiny hair, and a strong, supple physique. And taking care of yourself physically makes you *feel* beautiful from the outset.

🌀 *Find your style.* Maybe you love fashion and makeup; or maybe you thrive on wearing jeans and showing the world your unadorned face. Either can be beautiful. Find your style by making note of how you look when you feel most like yourself. You can dress up or down for specific occasions, but your basic style — romantic, tailored, exotic, whatever — will stay with you. Then you'll always feel comfortable about how you look, so you can forget about it and focus on what's really going on.

Don't get stuck. Some women get caught in a time warp: they pick a year and look like that for the rest of their lives. Without being a slave to trends, let your look gradually evolve to reflect the woman you are today.

Polish your soul. If you're healthy, well-groomed, and think well of your physical self, you'll look good, but to be truly beautiful, you have to be lit from within. This amazing, ageless glow comes from inside. Start with some quiet time; it will do as much for your face as a standing appointment at Elizabeth Arden. Do work you believe in, whether it's for love or money. Play with abandon. And smile a lot, so when you get lines on your face, they'll point up.

Victoria Moran

*Cheerfulness and content
are great beautifiers.*

Charles Dickens

I am beautiful.

Happiness is an essential part of my life. When I am happy, I feel incredibly alive. I feel at peace with myself and with the world. I try my best to find the lighter side of every situation and surround myself with people who keep my spirit inspired and uplifted. I am not the person who looks troubled or sad. I am the one who smiles for no reason and laughs extra loud.

I accept that there will be times when darkness overcomes me. With joy there will sometimes be sadness; with sunshine some rain will fall. It's okay for me to feel sad or angry sometimes. These emotions are a healthy part of life, but I will not allow them to linger long enough to dim my light. Emotions are contagious, and I will try my best to keep those around me feeling glad.

Today I will tell a joke to lighten the mood.

Today I will watch a funny movie.

Today I will bring happiness into every room I enter.

I Am Beautiful When...

I am beautiful when I laugh from deep down in my belly... when happiness rises up from inside me and touches every part of my being.

I am beautiful when I am smiling from ear to ear.

I am beautiful when I let my imagination take me to faraway places and beautiful adventures.

I am beautiful when I surround myself with nature.

*I am beautiful when my hands are deep in the soil
and I am one with the earth.*

*I am beautiful when I walk barefoot in the grass
and dance like a child in the sun.*

The most beautiful world is always enticed through the imagination.

Helen Keller

I am beautiful.

I remember how it felt to be a child… so young and carefree, so innocent and inspired. I remember how the world seemed an open canvas, how I chose my own colors and story lines. I remember how my imagination ran wild and I believed that anything was possible.

I will try my best to find that child within me. I know she is there waiting to make my world a better place. I will put on my rose-colored glasses each morning and try to keep them on throughout the day. My own inner beauty will help me to see the beauty in others. I won't take someone else's word for it. I will be an explorer, a creator, an artist. I will let my imagination take the reins. I will awaken the child within me and allow her to show me the way.

Today I will write with a bright-colored pen
instead of the usual blue or black.

Today I will finger-paint a picture of myself
using my favorite colors.

Today I will have a tea party.

We owe it to ourselves as women to cultivate our friendships, encourage each other's dreams, and understand our commonality. It is through these bonds that we find our true selves.

Lisa Crofton

I am beautiful.

I am most myself when I am surrounded by my friends. We nourish one another with kind words and laughter. We plead each other's cases and believe in each other's dreams. My friends provide me with strength and hope and love. I need them, and they need me.

When life gets hectic, I will make my friendships a main priority. I will let my friends nurture me when I feel distraught; I will lean on their shoulders when times are tough. I will create friendships that are built on companionship, support, and unconditional caring. True friendship is a beautifier of mind, body, and spirit. It completes my life and makes me beautiful.

Today I will contact someone I've lost touch with.

Today I will have coffee with an old friend.

Today I will send a friend a thank-you note.

Beauty is found in a calm spirit and a mind at peace.

Elle Mastro

I am beautiful.

Even superwomen need to take a break sometimes. It is my turn to step back and give myself a chance to breathe. If I feel overwhelmed, overworked, overstressed, or overtired, instead of moving forward, I will choose to stand still for a while. Only I am capable of knowing when my body and mind are running on empty. It is up to me to meet my own needs and treat myself with care.

This is my life, and I won't always be able to make everyone happy. I am not being selfish, but accepting reality. Taking care of myself will keep me healthy and strong. I will say no sometimes instead of squeezing it in. I will let the answering machine pick up once in a while. I will order dinner to go and use paper instead of glass, and I will go to bed early and press snooze in the morning. To be a better wife... mother... sister... daughter... woman, I first need to be a better me.

Today I will stay in bed one extra hour. Even if I am not tired, I will just let my body and mind relax.

Today I will draw myself a warm bath and soak by candlelight.

Today I will decline an invitation and not feel guilty.

I Am Beautiful When...

I am beautiful when I am fully present in the moment.

I am beautiful when I am surrounded by the people I love the most.

I am beautiful when I am a good role model for young girls and women and when I encourage them to be their best.

I am beautiful when I am passionate about the things that I do.

I am beautiful when I help carry the burden of someone who has a heavy heart.

I am beautiful when I share my wealth with someone less fortunate than me.

*L*ittle honesties, little passing words of sympathy, little nameless acts of kindness... these are the silent threads of gold which, when woven together, gleam out so brightly in the pattern of life.

Frederic W. Farrar

I am beautiful.

I am beautiful when I am kind and genuine. I am beautiful when I am friendly. I am beautiful when I reach out my hand to others to bless their lives with the gift of compassion.

My existence in this world makes a difference in the lives of those around me. Even when I feel weak or withdrawn from others, I must remember that my presence still holds great importance. My smile creates a circle of smiles. My laughter brings others a simple joy, and my company brings comfort to those I share my time with. I don't have to do something grandiose to make a difference. I just have to be me.

Today I will hold the door open for the person behind me.

Today I will share a funny story with someone.

Today I will smile at a stranger.

Beauty from Within

For attractive lips, speak words of kindness.

For lovely eyes, seek out the good in people.

For a slim figure, share your food with the hungry.

For beautiful hair, let a child run his or her fingers through it once a day.

For poise, walk with the knowledge you'll never walk alone.

People, even more than things, have to be restored, renewed, revived, reclaimed, and redeemed;
Never throw out anybody.

Remember, if you ever need a helping hand, you'll find it at the end of your arm.

As you grow older, you will discover that you have two hands, one for helping yourself, the other for helping others.

The beauty of a woman is not in the clothes she wears, the figure that she carries, or the way she combs her hair. The beauty of a woman must be seen from in her eyes, because that is the doorway to her heart, the place where love resides.

The beauty of a woman is not in a facial mole, but true beauty in a woman is reflected in her soul. It is the caring that she lovingly gives, the passion that she shows, and the beauty of a woman with passing years only grows!

Sam Levenson

There is the beauty of infancy,
the beauty of youth,
the beauty of maturity, and...
the beauty of age.

—— ⚘ ——

George Augustus Sala

I am beautiful.

As I grow older, my life goes through changes. I am not the same person I was ten years ago, and in ten years I will not be the same as I am now. My experiences over the years make me who I am today. I change and grow with each one. I will not fear what is to come with age, and I will not look back on my earlier years with envy. Each stage of my life offers me the chance to accept new roles, accomplish more feats, and grow more and more beautiful.

I will accept the years to come with grace. It won't always be easy. There will be changes I won't welcome — body parts that sag a bit and bones and muscles that ache on rainy days. But for the most part, it is my choice how the years affect me. I will take my time instead of rushing through life like I did in my earlier years. I will appreciate each day and let troubles roll off my shoulders. I will only be as old as I feel, and no matter how many birthdays pass, I will always feel beautiful.

Today I will take deeper breaths and slower steps.

Today I will bake myself a cake in celebration of being me.

*Today I will make a photo album with pictures
of myself from my birth until now.*

Beauty means caring for yourself.
Beauty means defining yourself.
Beauty means making the most
of what you've got.

Susan Kerr

I am beautiful.

There is one me in this world — one unique, extraordinary, beautiful me. I hold the utmost respect for myself — for my mind, body, and spirit. I do my best to treat myself with care and fill myself with only those things that have a positive effect on my life. My heart leads me to happiness, and I will try my best to follow that path.

I won't always make the right choices or have all the answers. I will make mistakes and life will go on; that is all I need to know. I will take chances and not fear what is to come. I will trust in myself and never give up. I am a courageous, intelligent, independent woman, and I am everything that is beautiful.

Today I will hold my head up high.

Today I will forgive myself for something I did or didn't do.

Today I will make a resolution… and keep it.

We Are Beautiful
Because We Are

The beauty of our bodies is not measured by the size we wear, but by the stories our bodies tell. We have tummies and hips that say, "I grew a child in here." We have hands that have cradled a new soul, wiped the brow of dying loved ones, picked flowers in the spring, touched the fragileness of a butterfly, and bandaged a wound.

We have hands we raise in worship; hands we gather in prayer; nails that may be bitten from worry; a callous that says, "I work hard."

The color of our skin tells who and where we came from; whether we baked in the sun or hid in the shade. Some of us have angel-kissed freckles.

We may have wrinkles, battle scars, or parts of
us missing — lost in a war of illness that we won
or are still fighting; signs of mischief and laughter
around our eyes — eyes that see, cry, and smile.
We may have dimples or clefts in our chins. We
have long arms or short arms, but still we reach.

We have long hair, short hair, no hair —
blond, brown, red, gray. It doesn't matter. Our
voices sing in tune or not — voices that scold and
comfort and share what's in our hearts. We may be
graceful or clumsy, short or tall, yet beautiful all.

We are beautiful because we are strong;
because when we love, we love deeply. The mirror
on the wall is only a reflection of the stories our
bodies tell. We are beautiful because we ARE.

Luanne Raavel

ACKNOWLEDGMENTS

We gratefully acknowledge the permission granted by the following authors, publishers, and authors' representatives to reprint poems or excerpts from their publications.

Randy House as representative of the Estate of Kaylan Pickford, for "I... do not know anyone..." and "Beautiful is connected to love..." from ALWAYS A WOMAN by Kaylan Pickford, published by Bantam Books. Copyright © 1982 by Kaylan Pickford and J. Frederick Smith. All rights reserved.

Sue Gillies-Bradley for "There Is So Much Beauty." Copyright © 2005 by Sue Gillies-Bradley. All rights reserved.

Random House, Inc., for "When a woman conceives..." from A WOMAN'S WORTH by Marianne Williamson. Copyright © 1993 by Marianne Williamson. All rights reserved.

Clarkson Potter/Publishers, an imprint of Random House, Inc., for "The best beauty product..." and "Beauty is in the eye of the beholder..." from THE ART OF IMPERFECTION by Véronique Vienne. Copyright © 1999 by Véronique Vienne. All rights reserved.

Crown Publishers, Inc., a division of Random House, Inc., for "Know your voice is your essential..." by Naomi Shihab Nye from HANDS ON!, edited by Suzanne Harper. Copyright © 2001 by Suzanne Harper. All rights reserved.

McGraw-Hill Education for "My mantra has become..." from WAKE-UP CALLS by Joan Lunden. Copyright © 2001 by New Life Entertainment, Inc. All rights reserved. And for "When my body is strong..." by Serena Williams from VENUS & SERENA: SERVING FROM THE HIP by Venus Williams and Serena Williams. Copyright © 2005 by Venus Williams and Serena Williams. All rights reserved.

G. P. Putnam's Sons, a division of Penguin Group (USA), Inc., for "It Has to Do..." from TRUE BEAUTY by Emme. Copyright © 1996 by Emme Associates, Inc. All rights reserved.

John Wiley & Sons, Inc., for "The ones who survive in life..." by Oprah Winfrey from OPRAH SPEAKS, edited by Janet Lowe. Copyright © 1988 by Janet Lowe. All rights reserved.

Brenda Hager for "Beautiful Women." Copyright © 2005 by Brenda Hager. All rights reserved.

HarperCollins Publishers for "Decide That You're Beautiful" from CREATING A CHARMED LIFE by Victoria Moran. Copyright © 1999 by Victoria Moran. All rights reserved.

Lisa Crofton for "We owe it to ourselves...." Copyright © 2005 by Lisa Crofton. All rights reserved.

SLL/Sterling Lord Literistic, Inc., for "Beauty from Within" from IN ONE ERA AND OUT THE OTHER by Sam Levenson. Copyright © 1973 by Sam Levenson. Reprinted by permission. All rights reserved.

Hodder Arnold for "Beauty means caring for yourself" from THE HEALTH & BEAUTY HANDBOOK by Susan Kerr. Copyright © 1997 by Susan Kerr. All rights reserved.

Luanne Raavel for "We Are Beautiful Because We Are." Copyright © 2005 by Luanne Raavel. All rights reserved.

A careful effort has been made to trace the ownership of selections used in this anthology in order to obtain permission to reprint copyrighted material and give proper credit to the copyright owners. If any error or omission has occurred, it is completely inadvertent, and we would like to make corrections in future editions provided that written notification is made to the publisher:

BLUE MOUNTAIN ARTS, INC., P.O. Box 4549, Boulder, Colorado 80306.